On 10 Feburary 1840 the most powerful woman in the world married a German prince who suddenly found himself at the very centre of history's greatest empire. But the sentiments Queen Victoria confided to her diary could have been those of any young wife who truly adored her new husband: 'Thank God! for me and others . . . I know what real happiness is.'

This is the story of that happiness, and of an enduring love that long survived the passing of its inspiration

Hulton-Deutsch Collection

BORN TO RULE

THE DISCIPLINED LIFE OF THE YOUNG PRINCESS
CONTRASTED SHARPLY WITH THE UPBRINGING OF HER
GERMAN COUSIN. ON VICTORIA'S 17TH BIRTHDAY, AT
ST JAMES'S PALACE, THE COUPLE MET FOR THE FIRST TIME

♛ *Within months of Victoria's birth, her father, the Duke of Kent below died. His premature death threw an awesome responsibility upon the future Queen's mother, the Duchess, who was determined to mould the young girl's character. Mother and child are shown right. Touchingly, Victoria is holding a miniature of her dead father*

By gracious permission of HM the Queen

By gracious permission of HM the Queen

TALK OF MARRIAGE BETWEEN THE YOUNG cousins, born only a few months apart in England and Germany, began when they were children. They had very different upbringings. Victoria's life in England was controlled from the moment she was born. As a child who was one day to be Queen, she was never allowed to be alone or choose her own friends. Albert's life in Germany was far more normal. After the initial shock of his mother leaving home, he and his brother Ernest happily mixed with other children and enjoyed their studies. The cousins met at a ball for Victoria's 17th birthday; she found him quite delightful, he enjoyed her company but was exhausted by her continuous merry-making. They were not to know that it would be three years before they met again and that the children from their subsequent union would shape the dynasties of Europe.

The young Victoria

The baby who was later to become Queen Victoria was born on 24 May 1819 at Kensington Palace after her mother, Princess Victoria of Saxe-Coburg, had had a precarious coach journey from Germany the previous day. The child was the result of an odd union. Her mother was a widow with two children and her father was the middle-aged Edward, Duke of Kent, son of the mad King George III, who was then nearing the end of his life with an ageing family of sons and no young heirs.

The Duke, along with his brothers, had been commanded to marry to secure the succession – and for him that meant leaving Julie, Madame de St Laurent, the unsuitable woman he had loved and lived with for 28 years. As he movingly told a friend, 'our unexpected separation arose from the imperative duty I owed to obey the call of my family and Country to marry, and not from the least diminution in attachment which had stood the test of 28 years and which, but for that circumstance, would unquestionably have kept up the connection, until it became the lot of one or other of us to be removed from the world'. His 'suitable' bride-to-be was also worried about giving up her comfortable independence but hoped to find compensation in the Duke's love.

From this unromantic start, a good marriage seemed to grow. Within a year of the wedding the 33-year-old Duchess and the 52-year-old Duke were the proud parents of the baby girl, delivered – unusually for those times – by a qualified female doctor, Fraulein Siebold.

The Duke of Kent was enchanted by his only child. 'The little girl is truly a model of

KENSINGTON PALACE

Princess Victoria found life at Kensington Palace rather dismal. As friends were not allowed, she had to learn to amuse herself, and her bedroom became a valued retreat, her dolls her only company. She kept the same bedroom throughout her childhood – it was there that she woke in 1837 to learn she had become Queen.

It was in this room too that she learned to sketch. She drew the appealing self-portrait *right* at the age of 13

Museum of London

By gracious permission of HM the Queen

strength and beauty combined,' he wrote. The only disappointment was that the Duke's brother, the Prince Regent, vetoed the baby's chosen names at the moment of christening, and she subsequently emerged with only two: Alexandrina Victoria.

Over in Germany

Just three months after Victoria was born, Fraulein Siebold was summoned to the Schloss Rosenau near Coburg in Germany, where, on 26 August 1819, she acted as midwife to the Duchess Louise, the young wife of the Duchess of Kent's brother, Duke Ernest. This boy, cousin to Victoria, was their second son. He was christened Francis Charles Augustus Albert Emmanuel – to be known by his family as Albert. He was 'a little squirrel with a pair of large black eyes', as his grandmother described him. Physically, the child was the spitting image of his beautiful mother, who was still only a young woman of 19.

♛ *The first recorded sketch of Albert, aged 9, shows how a cherubic look has been replaced with one of handsome arrogance*

Before Victoria had her first birthday, her apparently ever-fit father unexpectedly died of pneumonia, leaving his family penniless. Despite Victoria's proximity to the throne, no income was granted to her mother.

The family were rescued by Prince Leopold, the Duchess's brother, who made them an allowance on which they lived until 1825 when Parliament voted for a modest amount for Victoria's education and keep.

Victoria, with her half-sister Feodora from her mother's first marriage, and the Duchess then settled to a life of strict seclusion in their household at Kensington Palace. Victoria later remembered her childhood environment with horror. The palace was 'dreadfully dull, dark and gloomy' and populated with 'our Kensington friends, the black beetles'.

But it was not just the Palace itself that caused Victoria to shudder when she recalled her childhood. She had a miserable time, ruled over by two powerful and warring figures. One was Baroness Lehzen, the girls' governess, whom Victoria adored, but also feared. The other was the Comptroller for the Household, an Irish adventurer called Sir John Conroy. He was reputed to be her mother's lover and she trusted and relied upon him. To Victoria, he was a dreaded and hated figure, and she seemed instinctively to have spotted the faults to which her besotted mother was oblivious. He was an unscrupulous, scheming and officious man but had virile good looks and was unfailingly

> ## 'I am nearer to the throne than I thought . . . I will be good'
>
> ### PRINCESS VICTORIA

charming to the women he met.

In the young Victoria, Conroy saw his chance to become the most powerful man in England. With her mother willing to help him and follow all his advice, he prepared to educate and influence the future Queen from an early age so that when she took the throne he could rule through her. He instituted the 'Kensington system' – a strict regime of careful education. It was a policy that never allowed Victoria to be alone for a minute; it was planned to distance her from those at court, and to make her entirely dependent on her mother and Conroy.

The fact that Conroy never succeeded in his objectives is partly due to the fact that he never wooed and won over Victoria. She developed an implacable hatred towards him, and was supported in her dislike by Lehzen, who made sure that Victoria was never taken in by him. But Conroy, unfortunately, did succeed in turning her childhood into an extremely unhappy one.

Despite this, Victoria was essentially a bright child, with a strong personality and a will of her own. The qualities that were associated with her when she was Queen were apparent from her earliest years. She was almost disconcertingly honest and direct.

11 March 1830 was one of the most significant dates in Victoria's young life. It was decided that as she was nearly 11, it was time she knew the fact that one day she would be Queen. Her mother wanted her to learn of it in

SCHLOSS ROSENAU

Prince Albert was born and brought up in the Schloss Rosenau at Coburg in Germany. He and his brother Ernest had a disciplined childhood and were taught by their tutor, Florschütz, in this spartan room set in the roof of the house *below*. The boys slept in small bedrooms just off the main room

Kunstsammlungen Veste Coburg

the ordinary course of her lessons, so her teacher slipped an extra page into her history book showing the current line of succession. Victoria read it with anguish rather than pleasure. 'I am nearer to the throne than I thought,' she said, and burst into tears. She then made the famous vow: 'I will be good.'

Life continued as normal after this revelation, but Victoria continued to cry when she thought of her future. Her mother attended all Victoria's lessons, and even slept in her room. She accompanied Victoria and held her hand whenever she had to walk downstairs.

A sense of despair

Over the years, her resentment of Conroy's treatment of her began to spill over into her feelings for her mother, who always took his side. She came to feel suffocated and manipulated, relying more and more on the motherly

Baroness Lehzen, who always had her best interests at heart.

Her cousin, Prince Albert, also had a childhood that was less than serene. After his birth, Albert's parents started to drift apart. His father took several mistresses and neglected his young wife. She was beautiful and vivacious, and eventually also took comfort in the attentions of other men. In 1824, when Albert was five and his brother Ernest was six, Duke Ernest discovered that Louise was in love with a Lieutenant von Hanstein of the Coburg army. He forced her to leave home, and the children never saw her again. As Louise wrote in despair shortly afterwards, 'Leaving my children was the most painful thing of all . . . they had whooping cough and said "Mamma cries because she has got to go, now, when we are ill."'

Brotherhood

From around the time of their mother's departure, Albert and Ernest were looked after almost exclusively by a tutor. Although disciplined, Albert's childhood was much more normal and happy than Victoria's.

From an early age, Albert was counselled and guided by his uncle's physician, Baron Stockmar. The Baron was also to play an important part in later life when he became Albert's unofficial private secretary.

Like Victoria, Albert had an inclination to be serious, but hidden underneath was a wicked sense of fun. When he was three, his grandmother, the Dowager Duchess Augusta (who always hoped that Victoria and Albert would marry) wrote that he was 'lively, very funny, all good nature and full of mischief'.

Albert and Ernest were inseparable: they shared a room, studied together, and played together. The two Princes were also encouraged to play with the local children, which they did happily, without reminding them of their royal positions.

🔱 *Baron Christian Stockmar was an important figure in the Saxe-Coburg household. Although he cared for the family as a doctor, he also handled many of their legal affairs. When Prince Albert went to England, Baron Stockmar accompanied him as his unofficial private secretary*

Albert, it was said, loved to play practical jokes. His most spectacular effect was produced at the age of 11, when he scattered miniature glass stink-bombs on 'the floor of the pit and boxes of the theatre to the great annoyance and discomfiture of the audience, at whose confusion he was greatly delighted'.

As light relief, the boys were also encouraged to put on plays, and Albert, particularly, soon gained the reputation of a talented mimic. It was said that he had 'a great sense of the ludicrous, either in persons or in things; but he was never severe or ill-natured'.

But their studies, of course, always came first. They were given a strict and thoroughly well-balanced education, which included morality and religion. Albert grew up to be a serious, studious and thoughtful young man dedicated to the ideals of virtue, duty and self-sacrifice.

The cousins meet

Victoria, with her youthful inclination towards pleasure, would have been thrilled to have a life as varied and interesting as Albert's. When she was given the chance to enjoy herself, she did so with verve and delight. The King gave her a rare opportunity when she was 14, and he

THE BEGINNINGS OF LOVE

In 1836, Albert arrived in England for the first time accompanied by his brother Ernest. Victoria was in raptures over her cousin. Albert was less enthusiastic, commenting only that he found the heir to the throne 'amiable'

The Saxe-Coburg Link

Francis Frederick of Saxe-Saalfeld-Coburg
(1750-1806)

Ernest I — m. Louise of Saxe-Gotha-Altenburg
Duke of Saxe-Saalfeld-Coburg (1800-1831)
(1784-1844) div. 1826

Ernest II
Duke of Saxe-Coburg-Gotha
(1818-1893)

Albert, King m. Princess Alexandra
Edward VII of Denmark
(1841-1910) (1844-1925)

Prince Alfred m. Marie of Russia
Duke of Edinburgh and (1853-1920)
Saxe-Coburg-Gotha
(1844-1900)

Princess Victoria m. Frederick III,
(1840-1901) German Emperor and
King of Prussia
(1831-1888)

Princess Alice m. Louis IV, Grand
(1843-1878) Duke of Hesse-
Darmstadt
(1837-1892)

Princess Helena m. Prince Christian of
(1846-1923) Schleswig-Holstein
(1831-1917)

gave a ball for her birthday. She opened it on the arm of her cousin, Prince George, whom the King very much hoped she would marry. 'I was *very* much amused' she confided later in her diary.

In the spring of 1836, a more significant ball was given to celebrate Victoria's 17th birthday at Windsor. King William IV (who succeeded George IV in 1830) knew that Uncle Leopold, now King of the Belgians, was united with Victoria's mother and grandmother in hoping that Victoria would marry Albert. But William was opposed to the union and he tried unsuccessfully to stop them from coming to the ball. Victoria was very taken with her young German cousin, Albert. She impulsively reported in her diary 'the charm of his countenance is his expression which is most delightful; *c'est à la fois* full of goodness and sweetness, and very clever and intelligent'.

In a letter to Uncle Leopold she was similarly unrestrained: 'My cousins are delightful young people ... very kind and good, and extremely merry, just as young people should be; with all that, they are extremely sensible and very fond of occupation. Albert is extremely handsome.'

Victoria's enthusiasm was not dimmed by the fact that Albert, unused to late nights, was so exhausted by the day of the ball that he almost collapsed and had to retire early. In truth, he was rather appalled by Victoria's enthusiasm for parties and late nights.

Although both young people knew that those around them hoped they would marry, nothing was ever said. Albert returned home, and in 1837 he went to Bonn university. He distinguished himself as a student and was a good all-rounder: he was a prize-winning fencer, took part in concerts and acted in amateur theatricals. He was an outstandingly handsome young man according to the fashion of the day, but his name was never linked with a woman's.

The start of a new era

That same year, in May 1837, Victoria turned 18 and, just over a month later in the early hours of 20 June, King William IV died, suffocated by asthma. At six o'clock in the morning the household at Kensington Palace was rudely awakened by the Archbishop of Canterbury and the Lord Chamberlain. Young Victoria, with her hair loose and wearing only a dressing gown, was brought down to see them and was hailed as the new Queen.

Fotomas Index

⚜ *On 20 June 1837, Victoria was awakened by the Archbishop of Canterbury and the Lord Chamberlain to be told that she was now Queen*

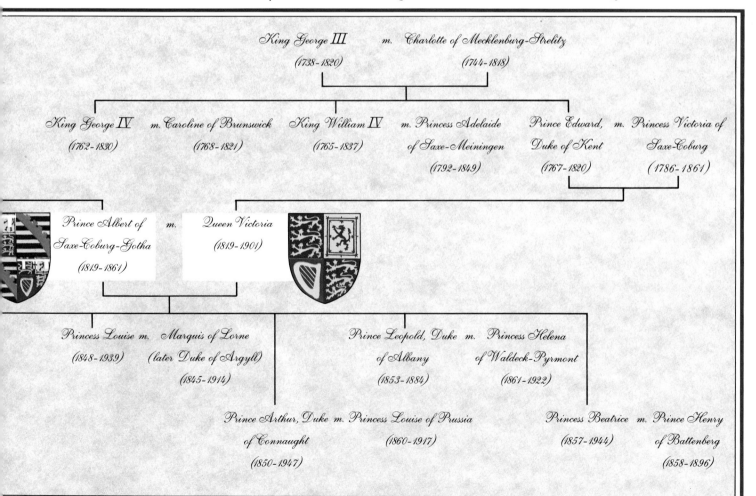

King George III (1738-1820) m. Charlotte of Mecklenburg-Strelitz (1744-1818)

King George IV (1762-1830) m. Caroline of Brunswick (1768-1821)

King William IV (1765-1837) m. Princess Adelaide of Saxe-Meiningen (1792-1849)

Prince Edward, Duke of Kent (1767-1820) m. Princess Victoria of Saxe-Coburg (1786-1861)

Prince Albert of Saxe-Coburg-Gotha (1819-1861) m. Queen Victoria (1819-1901)

Princess Louise (1848-1939) m. Marquis of Lorne (later Duke of Argyll) (1845-1914)

Prince Leopold, Duke of Albany (1853-1884) m. Princess Helena of Waldeck-Pyrmont (1861-1922)

Prince Arthur, Duke of Connaught (1850-1947) m. Princess Louise of Prussia (1860-1917)

Princess Beatrice (1857-1944) m. Prince Henry of Battenberg (1858-1896)

VIVAT REGINA

Designed especially for Victoria, the Imperial State Crown forms the centrepiece of her regalia. But when the young Queen was crowned, there was a host of other Crown Jewels on display: from the small crown she loved and preferred to wear, to the Coronation ring, anointing objects and the magnificent Sovereign's orb

THE AMPULLA

Made in the form of an eagle, the Ampulla holds the holy oil used in the Ceremony of Anointing at the Coronation. It was first used for the Coronation of King Charles II in 1661

THE ANOINTING SPOON

Dating from the 12th century, the spoon was used to anoint the newly crowned Queen with holy oil from the Ampulla

British Crown copyright reproduced with the permission of the controller of HMSO

ILN Picture Library

THE ORB

Like the Ampulla, the Sovereign's orb dates from the Coronation of King Charles II. It is a hollow gold sphere six and a half inches in diameter and weighing three pounds. It is richly ornamented with pearls and precious stones

THE IMPERIAL STATE CROWN

The crown was made for Queen Victoria in 1837 and features almost 2800 jewels. The cross contains the Black Prince's ruby and was worn by King Henry V at the Battle of Agincourt in 1415. Immediately below it is the 104-carat Stuart sapphire. A second large sapphire is said to come from the ring of King Edward the Confessor. The large drop pearls came from earrings belonging to Queen Elizabeth I

THE SMALL CROWN

Queen Victoria found the Imperial State Crown was too heavy for her and in 1870 this smaller crown was made for State occasions. Weighing only four ounces and less than four inches high, it contained over 2300 diamonds

THE CORONATION RING

Given to Victoria by her mother, the Duchess of Kent, the ring comprises a ruby cross set in sapphire, surrounded by diamonds

LONG MAY SHE REIGN

VICTORIA WAS CROWNED QUEEN AT 19. TWO YEARS LATER, SHE HAD FALLEN IN LOVE WITH THE PRINCE WITH WHOM SHE WAS TO SHARE THE THRONE

THE NATION WAS CHARMED BY THEIR NEW, young Queen. Barely five feet tall, with a slim, slight build, Victoria, at her accession, was the prettiest she would ever be, with her clear complexion, large blue eyes and wavy light brown hair. It was not only the people who were taken with her; Victoria delighted the cynical Privy Councillors who assembled for the first council of her reign. Her looks and her shyness mixed with a regal confidence were an utterly beguiling combination. She entered the room in a black dress, 'of course quite *alone*' as she said later in her diary – she had entirely thwarted the attempts of Conroy and her mother to have any influence on her at all now she was Queen. Indeed, Victoria's first action as Queen was to have her mother's bed removed from her room.

At that council, Victoria was greeted by her two uncles, the Dukes of Cumberland and Sussex, and was led to the throne where she read her declaration in a clear voice.

The Coronation

Victoria was crowned Queen on 28 June 1838 in Westminster Abbey. She slept badly the night before, but the most popular monarch for decades was thrilled by the reception of the crowds. Victoria entered the Abbey wearing the Parliament Robes of crimson velvet, trimmed with ermine and gold lace and fastened with a golden cord. She was attended by eight train-bearers.

The Coronation ceremony itself was not without hitches. One mistake was significant in view of an old legend about the Coronation ring – 'the closer the fit the longer the reign'. Much to Victoria's agony, the aged Archbishop of Canterbury forced the ruby ring on to her fourth finger, not noticing it had been made for her fifth. That evening, she only managed to re-move the ring after bathing her finger in iced water – but the prophesy came true.

The new Queen

After Victoria moved to Buckingham Palace, her adored 'mother' Lehzen was effectively in charge, handling all the staff and controlling Victoria's dazzling privy purse of £60,000 per year. Victoria also relied heavily on the advice and support of her Prime Minister, Lord Melbourne. At 58, he was old enough to be her grandfather, and indeed she began to look on him as her father, supplanting even the adored uncle Leopold in her affections. Although he was elderly, Melbourne was a handsome and distinguished man, and he was charming, witty and knowledgeable as well. Victoria's diary was full of comments about him: what he did, said and looked like. He was, she said, 'the

♛ *The five-hour Coronation ceremony on 28 June 1838 was a great ordeal for the young Victoria. Many mistakes were made by the celebrants, but she bore up bravely and left the Abbey triumphantly. Public joy was reflected in a vast selection of mass-produced memorabilia*

best-hearted, kindest and most feeling man in the world'. He returned her warm affection in full, treating her almost as a daughter, but with the respect due to a Queen. As a young girl, she had had so few people to love her or to lavish her own affectionate nature on, and when she found someone worthy, she responded with generous-hearted warmth.

When Lord Melbourne's government faced defeat in the Commons in 1839, he advised her that she must choose a new Prime Minister from the opposition. She hated the Tories and had once naively stated that she thought the monarch should always be a Whig – as was Lord Melbourne and his party. At the thought of losing her dear adviser, she wept profusely. She also stood firm against Melbourne's suggested successor, Sir Robert Peel, when he wanted her principal ladies-in-waiting to be changed to include

some Tories – an accepted convention at that time.

Victoria's vehement opposition to letting any of her ladies go made it impossible for Peel to form a government, and Melbourne was obliged to stay in office. With hindsight Victoria agreed she had acted badly, 'but I was *very* young . . . and never should have acted so again'.

The diarist Charles Greville, his first favourable impression of the new Queen now tarnished, had another interpretation of Victoria's animosity towards Peel and Tories in general. 'The simple truth is that the Queen could not endure the thought of parting with Melbourne, who is everything to her. Her feelings, which are *sexual* though she does not know it and are probably not very well defined to herself, are of a strength sufficient to tear down all prudential considerations.'

Certainly, Victoria had often described herself as 'naturally very passionate'. By that,

♛ *HM Queen Victoria, 28 June 1837*

LORD MELBOURNE

As Queen, Victoria came to rely heavily on the advice of her Prime Minister. He was a handsome man, and her attachment to him caused much gossip. Shown above is one of several sketches she drew of him

By gracious permission of HM the Queen

she meant that she had an uncontrollable temper, and that when she was happy, she enjoyed herself to the full.

Time to marry

Victoria was a girl who had known little affection, but had a great capacity for love and longed to be able to give it properly. She was a young girl, who had had little fun and who had never had the thrill of being courted. The first intoxicating excitement of being Queen had worn off, to be replaced by a prospect that was not at all pleasant – she had lost her popularity and years of ruling stretched in front of her. If ever a girl was ready to fall in love and to contemplate marriage, it was Victoria.

She did not want an arranged marriage and, although she had looked favourably on Albert when she had met him a few years before, it was no longer enough that her family wished them to marry.

In October 1839, Albert and Ernest were due to visit England and the new Queen. Albert had heard that Victoria was no longer so interested in marrying him. Victoria had written to her Uncle Leopold: 'I may not have the feeling for him which is requisite to ensure happiness. I may like him as a friend, and as a cousin and a brother.'

Albert, who had spent the last few years believing that they would one day be married, was piqued and worried. If Victoria did not make up her mind for years, he might well be unable to make a worthy marriage with another royal princess.

Albert came over to London with the 'quiet but firm resolution to declare that I also, tired of the delay, withdrew from the affair'.

FALLING IN LOVE

Albert and Ernest arrived at Windsor Castle on 10 October 1839 in the early evening. Albert was white and shaken from their turbulent passage, and their clothes had gone astray so they had nothing to change into for dinner. They were not able to join the others, and dined in their rooms alone. Victoria, who a few months before had told Melbourne that she had 'no great wish to see Albert', found that the sight of him was marvellously disturbing. The last time she had seen her cousins, they were young boys – now they were grown up and had changed out of all recognition.

The next day, her first impression was wonderfully reinforced. Albert was an extraordinarily good-looking man and, at five foot seven inches, tall in comparison to herself. 'Albert is really quite charming,' she wrote excitedly. He was also 'excessively handsome, such beautiful blue eyes, an exquisite nose, and such a pretty mouth with delicate moustachios and slight, but very slight, whiskers; a beautiful figure, broad in the shoulders and fine waist; my heart is quite going'. Everything about him seemed to please: 'It is quite a pleasure to look at Albert when he gallops and waltzes, he does it so beautifully, holds himself so well with that beautiful figure of his.'

Victoria felt bound to tell her dear friend Melbourne that seeing Albert had made her change her mind about marrying. As early as 14 October, Victoria had made up her mind – she was in love, and she wanted to marry Albert. She had been unable to sleep with excitement since his arrival, and she had heard that he was similarly disturbed. The problem remained to tell him of her decision.

The next day, Victoria sent for Albert. As she said later, Albert 'would never have presumed to take such a liberty to propose to the Queen of England'. She received him in her little blue boudoir, and there, trembling as she spoke, she proposed.

She wrote, 'I told him … it would make me too *happy* if he would consent to what I wished. We embraced each other over and over again, and he was *so* kind, *so* affectionate; Oh! to *feel* I was, and am, loved by *such* an Angel as Albert was *too great a delight* to describe! He is *perfection;* perfection in every way – in beauty – in everything! I told him I was quite unworthy of him … he said

Fotomas Index

♛ *When Albert returned to England the royal affair started in earnest. The couple were always chaperoned to public places such as the opera above. Moments alone were rare – and were always in the open*

Hulton-Deutsch Collection

he would be very happy … and was so kind and seemed so happy, that I felt it was the happiest brightest moment in my life, which made up for all I had suffered and endured.'

Albert, who had been waiting with some trepidation for the proposal, was very pleased that all was now resolved. But, unlike Victoria, it had not been important to him that the marriage should be a love match. While Victoria's feelings were all romantic, Albert's had a different stamp. 'I will not let my courage fail,' he wrote. 'With firm resolution and true zeal on my part, I cannot fail to continue noble, manly and princely in all things.'

'With the exception of my relations towards Victoria', he continued, 'my future position will have its dark sides, and the sky will not always be blue and unclouded.'

But to find that his bride-to-be was an attractive and adoring young girl was an unlooked-for bonus.

By gracious permission of HM the Queen

The next couple of weeks were spent in a dream as far as Victoria was concerned. The delight of being able to express her love, and be shown such affection in return, intoxicated her.

A wonderful courtship

Dreading his departure, she begged for a piece of Albert's hair to be treasured when he was gone, and charted every second of the time they spent together. 'At seven minutes past six came my most beloved Albert and stayed with me till ten minutes past seven. He was so affectionate, so kind, so dear, we kissed each other again and again. We sit so nicely side by side on that little blue sofa; no two lovers could ever be happier than we are! He took my hands in his and said that my hands were so little he could hardly believe they were hands, as he had hitherto only been accustomed to handle hands his brother like Ernest's.'

It was the fact that Albert had never been in love, and never even looked at another woman, that crowned Victoria's happiness.

THE COURTSHIP

Albert and Victoria shared a mutual love of music and, during Albert's visit, the young lovers would spend many evenings at the piano, with Victoria playing and both of them singing Albert's pencilled compositions. He was also a graceful dancer, an accomplishment which Victoria had discovered and greatly admired on his previous visit. Many informal dances were held at Kensington Palace, where Albert happily indulged Victoria's passion for enjoying herself by waltzing with her into the early hours of the morning

John Johnson Collection/Bodleian Library

Her Majesty.   (————) Duchess, of Kent. Duke, of Sussex.

All too soon, this romantic idyll was over. On 14 November 1839, Albert had to return to Coburg to prepare for the coming wedding. When he left, Victoria wept into her journal. 'We kissed each other so often, and I leant on that dear soft cheek, fresh and pink like a rose … It was ten o'clock and it was the time for his going … I gave Albert a last kiss, and saw him get into his carriage and drive off. I cried so much, felt wretched, yet happy to think that we should meet again so soon! Oh! how I love him, how intensely, how devotedly, how ardently! I cried and felt so sad.'

On 23 November, the Queen gave the news of her engagement to the Privy Council. Charles Greville wrote afterwards, 'The Queen came in, attired in a plain morning gown, but wearing a bracelet containing Prince Albert's picture. She read the declaration in a clear, sonorous, sweet-toned voice but her hands trembled so excessively that I wonder she was able to read the paper which she held.'

> *'I told him … it would make me too happy if he would consent … We embraced each other over and over again, and he was so kind, so affectionate'*
>
> QUEEN VICTORIA ON HER ENGAGEMENT

Victoria was soon angered by the reception Albert was given by the House of Commons. One of their first duties was to vote him a regular annuity. The usual figure to be given was £50,000, but the Exchequer was in financial trouble, and it was felt that this was far too much. The sum was reduced to £30,000 after a Tory member put in an amendment. This action reinforced Queen Victoria's hatred for all things Tory.

When he heard the news, Albert was more philosophical. He regretted the loss of income mainly because it would mean he would have less money to use as patron of the arts.

The second blow came when Victoria asked for Albert to be granted precedence second only to her in the country. Her royal uncles demurred – it would mean that he came before them in importance, and this too was strongly refused.

The fact that Albert was a foreigner, and young at that, was not well received generally. *The Times* wrote: 'One might, without being unreasonable, express a wish that the consort selected for … Queen Victoria should have been a person of riper years, and likely to form more sound and circumspect opinions.'

But although Albert was young, he was a serious person and in many ways brilliant. Even Victoria, dazzled as she was by Albert's beauty, and utterly in love with being in love, had not yet realized quite what an excellent man she had chosen to be her husband. She waited his return with impatience, and when he did all the recent unpleasantness was forgotten.

♔ *It was Victoria's prerogative as Queen to propose marriage to Prince Albert. This she did in her intimate little room, the Blue Closet, on 15 October 1839. Albert accepted and, the tension broken, they fell into each other's arms*

Albert will you marry me?

Orange blossom, scattered with diamonds

Honiton Lace veil 1½ yards square

♛ The bride wears a wreath of orange blossom, discreetly studded with a handful of sparkling diamonds

♛ Victoria, aged 16. The shape of her dress has become traditional for modern ballet costumes. The waistline is high and embroidery at knee level breaks the length of the skirt. The hair is elaborately stiffened

Full-gathered skirt supported by petticoats

Deep flounce of antique Honiton lace

ROYAL FASHION

THE AGE OF THE CRINOLINE

The crinoline shape is always associated with Queen Victoria but, in fact, skirt shapes evolved throughout her reign, from ample fullness in 1837 to a huge circumference by the 1850s. The many supporting petticoats were reinforced with horsehair – called 'crin' in French – hence the word crinoline. Sadly, the death of Albert brought Victoria's interest in fashion to an end. She wore perpetual mourning and ignored further fashion changes

Turkish
diamond
necklace and
earrings

♔ The wedding dress was in white satin with a deep flounce of Honiton lace. The sleeves were gathered into puffs above the elbow and the bodice was deeply pointed at the waist. The satin train was 18 feet long. The chain of the Garter completed the ensemble

Low décolletage permissible for wedding ceremony

♔ Prince Albert wore the scarlet and white uniform of a British Field Marshal, with bridal favours at his shoulder. His star and riband of the Order of the Garter were given to him the night before the wedding

♛ This bonnet was worn by Victoria in 1837. The large stiffened brim and high crown followed the fashion of the day

Frilled half sleeves

By gracious permission of HM the Queen

♛ A formal portrait by Winterhalter, painted in 1842, shows how the skirt has perceptibly widened. It is supported by layers of petticoats. The shoulders are bared, but the ankles discreetly covered

Crisp silk without any pattern

Fresh camellias used for trimming at neck, sleeves and on skirt

Ribbon trimming arranged in lace-up effect

♛ When she was young, Victoria loved to dance, and this off-the-shoulder ballgown is typically appealing. She wore flowers in her hair and flat-soled satin slippers

Two-tier flounce to skirt

White lace collar

Brilliantly striped waistcoat with wide lapels

👑 By the 1850s, hair was flat on top, smoothed low over the ears with a bun at the nape of the neck. Soft lace caps like this followed the contour of the hair

Fine cashmere shawl

Flounced skirt with horizontal ribbon border

👑 Albert's dark suit shows how the flamboyant men's clothes of Regency days were replaced by Victorian sobriety. His striped waistcoat and watch chain are the only touches of fashion still permissible

👑 The crinoline was at its widest by 1861. This dress also shows the great popularity of checks and horizontal trimmings. Little lace collars and wide pagoda sleeves with matching undersleeves were popular for daytime wear. A shawl was frequently worn

VICTORIA. ALBERT.

HAPPY AND GLORIOUS

AFTER THEIR WEDDING, VICTORIA WAS BLISSFULLY HAPPY. ALBERT, HOWEVER, WAS FRUSTRATED BY HIS LACK OF POLITICAL INFLUENCE. THE ARRIVAL OF THEIR CHILDREN PROVIDED A PERIOD OF GLORIOUS FULFILMENT

A T THE BEGINNING OF FEBRUARY 1840, Albert and his family arrived in England after yet another stormy sea crossing that left the Prince prostrate in his cabin.

He arrived at the Palace on 8 February, still not quite recovered from his sea-sickness. Victoria, beside herself with excitement, bestowed the Order of the Garter on him and gave him a diamond star and badge – all before dinner. Lord Melbourne joked about being ignored now that the glamorous groom had arrived, and made them all laugh by insisting that they admire his new coat for a while.

The day of the wedding, Monday 10 February 1840, dawned with torrents of rain and violent gusts of wind. Victoria dashed off a tender note to Albert. 'How are you today, and have you slept well? I have rested very well, and feel very comfortable today. What weather! I believe, however, the rain will cease. Send one word when you, my most dearly loved bridegroom, will be ready. Thy ever-faithful, Victoria R.'

London was packed with sightseers ready to cheer the attractive young couple. Victoria and Albert were to be married in the Chapel Royal, St James's Palace. Victoria drove there in a carriage with her mother and the Duchess of Sutherland beside her. 'I never saw such crowds of people as there were in the Park, and they cheered most enthusiastically,' she wrote.

At St James's, her 12 train-bearers waited, 'dressed all in white with white roses, which had a beautiful effect'.

The wedding service

The bridegroom was ushered in to Handel's tune *See the conqu'ring hero comes!* and then Victoria arrived on the arm of her uncle, the Duke of Sussex, who was to give her away. She would always remember the moment: 'The Flourish of Trumpets ceased as I entered the Chapel, and the organ began to play, which had a beautiful effect.'

Victoria looked young and vulnerable in her white satin dress. Albert, with his fine figure, looked incredibly handsome. He wore the uniform of a British Field Marshal, as well as the diamond Order of the Garter Victoria had given him days before.

Victoria found the marriage service very moving: 'Very imposing, and fine and simple, and I think ought to make an everlasting impression on every one who promises at the altar to keep what he or she promises.' Significantly, one of Victoria's vows was to obey. The best moment, though, was when Albert slipped the ring on. 'I felt so happy when the ring was put on, and by Albert.'

A large crowd cheered the couple in St James's Park. When they left Buckingham Palace for their honeymoon, more cheers followed them on their way to Windsor.

The wedding of Queen Victoria and Prince Albert at the Chapel Royal, St James's Palace, attracted large crowds who, despite the wind and rain, gathered to cheer the royal couple along their route. The ceremony was followed by a banquet at Buckingham Palace, where guests enjoyed a cake weighing 300 pounds. Articles such as this jug and medal were issued to commemorate the occasion

HER MAJESTY'S BRIDAL CAKE.

Museum of London

Hulton-Deutsch Collection

Private Collection/Bridgeman Art Library

By gracious permission of HM the Queen

⚜ *The birth of Princess Victoria in 1840*

BIRTH OF A DYNASTY

The subject of the honeymoon had been a vexed one. Albert had expected, and suggested, a honeymoon of a decent length. But Victoria had let him know her feelings in a letter before he returned to England for the wedding. She believed that a honeymoon of two or three days at Windsor would be plenty. She wrote to him as his future Queen, rather than bride: 'You forget, my dearest Love, that I am the Sovereign, and that business can stop for nothing.'

Victoria was unbelievably happy the evening of their wedding day. But the strain of the excitement finally told. By dinnertime she had a sick headache.

The next day it was Albert's turn to feel ill, but it had started perfectly: 'When day dawned (for we did not sleep much) and I beheld that beautiful angelic face by my side, it was more than I can express! He does look so beautiful in his shirt only, with his beautiful throat seen.'

It did not seem possible that she could be happier, but the next day, she was in even greater ecstasies. 'Already the second day since our marriage; his love and gentleness is beyond everything, and to kiss that dear soft cheek, to press my lips to his, is heavenly bliss. I feel a purer more unearthly feel than I ever did! Oh! was ever woman so blessed as I am?'

Everything was charming. If the sexual side of marriage had held any fears for Victoria she

> ## 'His love and gentleness is beyond everything . . . Oh was ever woman so blessed as I am?'
>
> VICTORIA ON HER HONEYMOON

was soon reassured.

On the last day of the honeymoon she wrote with pride, 'My dearest Albert put my stockings on for me.' And then, with the excitement and pleasure of a girl who had never known her own father, she added, 'I went in and saw him shave; a great delight for me.'

In three days, the honeymoon was over. The briefness of it caused talk and a considerable amount of comment. The political diarist Charles Greville was shocked at their early rising: 'This was not the way to provide us with a Prince of Wales,' he said sourly.

Early difficulties for Albert

There was no doubt that Victoria was entranced by her new husband, but the attitude of others was less welcoming. Officially he was all but snubbed. At court he was also less than popular: despite his good looks, his manner was stiff, and his thick German accent was thought to be off-putting.

Married life was also proving to be somewhat stormy. Despite the fact that during the marriage ceremony Victoria had promised to obey, Albert was finding problems with her imperious manner. On one dramatic occasion after an argument, Albert locked himself in his room, while Victoria beat upon the door to be let in. 'Who is it?' asked Albert. 'The Queen of England', said Victoria. No movement or sound from inside. After the question had been repeated, Victoria answered in a more subdued manner, 'Your wife, Albert.' At that the door opened at once.

If it was hard for Victoria to remember that within their household she was Albert's wife rather than his Queen, it was impossible for her to forget that for all other purposes she ruled.

At first she would not let him have any say in political business. She told him kindly that all she expected was a little 'help with the blotting paper'. Not only that, Victoria bossily organized his official life to such an extent that she chose all the officers of Albert's household,

By gracious permission of HM the Queen

⚜ *Edwin Landseer's painting, Windsor Castle in Modern Times, was commissioned by Victoria in 1841 for the Prince's birthday. The growing influence of Albert on Victoria is reflected in the way she stands demurely beside her husband, while baby Princess Victoria plays with the family dogs. Over the years, Victoria came to share Albert's pleasure in the countryside and Windsor became an increasingly relaxing retreat*

By gracious permission of HM the Queen

👑 **Albert is shown** above *in 1842 wearing the Order of the Garter, a gift from Victoria just before their wedding. By now, his position was* *more secure, having rid Victoria of the influence of Baroness Lehzen. The Baroness is shown below, sketched by Victoria*

By gracious permission of HM the Queen

including his confidential secretary – who had previously worked for the Prime Minister, Lord Melbourne. Victoria told Albert that she had taken advice from Melbourne and that he was to trust her.

Albert begged to be allowed to choose his own men. Victoria would not give in. But Albert was clever and subtle. He knew there was no point in pressing the issue then – and he knew he had time. Meanwhile at least his valet was his own choice – Cart, who had been with him since he was seven.

Until Albert was able to involve himself fully in the affairs of state, he concentrated his attentions on making sure that things ran smoothly for Victoria. He began by rationalizing the domestic arrangements at all the royal residences, which he found in a hopeless muddle, concentrating in particular on their conspicuous waste and over-generous perks.

He insisted, for example that any left-over bread be given to the really needy rather than taken home by well-paid royal servants. But his economies were pilloried: caricatures of him showed the Prince ferreting like a tramp for candle-ends in palatial surroundings.

Albert's guiding hand

Albert soon realized that before he would be able to assert himself politically, he would have to have the full confidence of the Queen – and that was impossible given the hold that Baroness Lehzen still had over her, both financially and emotionally. It took time – two years – before Albert's influence over Victoria matched or exceeded Lehzen's, but it was inevitable that it would. When it did, Albert was able tactfully to get rid of Lehzen by sending her on a recuperative 'holiday' from which she never returned to duty.

Albert's influence on Victoria politically began to have effect from the time their first child was

♛ *Christmas was a favourite time for Albert and was always spent at Windsor. Candle-lit trees were set up in the Queen's and the Prince's rooms and in another room for the children*

♛ *The christening of the heir to the throne. Albert Edward, the Prince of Wales, was baptized in St George's Chapel, Windsor. Victoria later wrote that the best thing about the future King was that he now had his dear father's name*

Many happy moments were spent away from London. Christmas, in particular, was a marvellous time, such as Victoria had never experienced as a child. It was always spent at Windsor and they made everything as exciting as they could.

Both Victoria and Albert loved Scotland, too, and particularly Balmoral where they could forget for weeks at a time that they were royal. In all this, Albert's influence was clear to see. In a relatively short space of time he had managed to turn Victoria from a dedicated town person into a country-lover, who longed for the peace and fresh air of life outside London.

Contrary to the general views held about Albert, he *did* know how to enjoy himself, particularly when young and first married, before he became overwhelmed with affairs of state. His sense of humour was either literary – he liked making puns and inventing riddles – or slapstick. He continued to enjoy practical jokes, although he usually confined himself to making them on April Fool's day. For all his seriousness, Albert could laugh at himself too. He collected cartoons and caricatures, especially those of which he was the butt.

Albert's good looks had initially been a source of excitement among the ladies of the court, but they soon found his manner icy cold in its lack of interest. In fact, Albert found women difficult to get along with – he never learnt to flirt, partly because he had no inclination to do so. Victoria was delighted by his manner with other women, and talked with satisfaction of his 'utter indifference at the attraction of all ladies'.

Happy family life

Although there was no doubt that to begin with Victoria was more in love with Albert than he with her, his manner was tenderness itself, and over the years his love for her deepened. One of the children's governesses noted that 'it was very pleasant to find him reading aloud to her while she waited, doing her cross-stitch, for one of the ladies to come in to dress her for dinner'. She concluded 'oh what a blessing it was that love ruled the court'.

The royal princes and princesses often had great fun with their parents. This was mainly Albert's influence. He remembered a childhood that was studded with happy moments and childlike pleasure. Both Victoria and Albert enjoyed crawling on the floor with the babies, or helping the older children build snowmen. Later they organized *tableaux vivants* and amateur theatricals for the children to take part in. Albert was even seen to demonstrate the

born. The Princess Royal, Victoria Adelaide, was born on 22 November 1840. Little Vicky was to become Albert's favourite child, but the first service she did him was to allow Victoria to release some of her work into Albert's hands. It was noticed that while Victoria was confined after giving birth, the ministerial boxes were sent to her anyway and were dealt with as usual – but now it was Albert's guiding hand that took charge. Soon after Vicky's birth, Victoria was pregnant again, and on 9 November 1841 Albert Edward, the Prince of Wales, was born. Victoria spent much of the following years pregnant and recovering from labour. Seven more children were to follow: Alice in 1843, Alfred in 1844, Helena in 1846, Louise in 1848, Arthur in 1850, Leopold in 1853, and Beatrice in 1857. During all this time Victoria was grateful to have Albert to help her. For she became more and more convinced that Albert's judgements were brilliant, and that whatever he decided was right.

Charles Greville was one of many people to notice the change. 'It is obvious,' he observed, 'that, while she has the title, he is really discharging the functions of Sovereign.'

Shared interests

It was not just in affairs of state that Albert had his influence. He was better educated than Victoria, and his mind was more sensitive and subtle. Gradually, he began to communicate his knowledge and enthusiasm to her and they came to share several interests, such as art and music.

correct way to do a somersault. Victoria, typically, enjoyed organizing parties for the children, but otherwise did not get the same pleasure from them that Albert did. Unlike other mothers, her children never came to mean more to her than her husband: 'I only feel properly *à mon aise* and quite happy when Albert is with me', she wrote to a friend.

As with everything Albert did, she admired his dealings with the children enormously. 'He romps with them so delightfully', she wrote, 'and manages them so beautifully and firmly.'

Those who knew Albert well noticed that he tried to treat his children as equals. Consequently they grew to love him dearly, as his wife did. In many ways this love match was idyllic. Victoria believed that it was so good and perfect that it would last forever, and she prayed that she would die before her beloved Albert – or, at the very least, not have the pain of surviving him.

By gracious permission of HM the Queen

👑 *Over the years Victoria and Albert grew increasingly devoted to one another, with the Prince in particular deriving enormous pleasure in family life. The royal couple would often commission and exchange pictures of the children as gifts, and sketched them in idle moments, as shown in this drawing* left *of Prince Albert (later Edward VII) aged nine, by Victoria. The memorable portrait of Victoria and Albert and the Royal Family* below *was painted in 1846. The couple were to have four more children*

♔ *Prince Albert looks lovingly on the two-year-old Princess Victoria*

♔ *Prince Arthur, aged seven, in guardsman's uniform*

♔ *Prince Arthur left and Prince Alfred at Osborne, in the costumes of Sikh Princes, 1854*

♔ *Princess Victoria left and Princess Alice, 1855*

♔ *Victoria, Princess Royal, aged 15, at Osborne*

♔ *Princess Helena foreground and Princess Louise at Osborne, 1854*

Hulton-Deutsch Collection

Caldesi

Dr E Becker

Roger Fenton

J/E Mayall

Dr E Becker

Roger Fenton

👑 *Princess Helena* right *and Princess Louise, 1855*

👑 *Victoria's mother, the Duchess of Kent, with Princess Victoria and the future Edward VII*

Family Album

The children of Victoria & Albert

👑 *Queen Victoria with Princess Beatrice, aged four*

Hulton-Deutsch Collection

Caldesi

👑 *Prince Arthur, aged seven*

Caldesi

👑 *The Royal Family at Osborne, May 1857*

All photographs except Hulton-Deutsch Collection by gracious permission of HM the Queen

ROYAL RESIDENCE

OSBORNE HOUSE

Osborne House, on the Isle of Wight, was purchased in 1844 and redesigned by Prince Albert, helped by the famous London builder, Thomas Cubitt. Many of the happiest days of Queen Victoria's life were spent there, relaxing with her young family and enjoying the local bathing and boating. Some of her saddest times were spent at Osborne, too, when she retired there after her husband's death. Every detail was kept unchanged

English Heritage

English Heritage

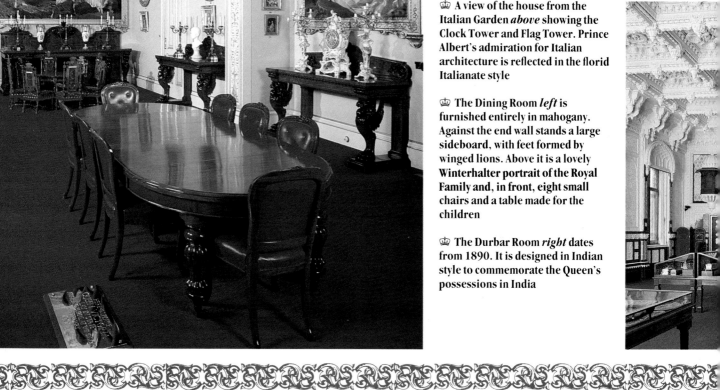

♛ A view of the house from the Italian Garden *above* showing the Clock Tower and Flag Tower. Prince Albert's admiration for Italian architecture is reflected in the florid Italianate style

♛ The Dining Room *left* is furnished entirely in mahogany. Against the end wall stands a large sideboard, with feet formed by winged lions. Above it is a lovely **Winterhalter portrait of the Royal Family** and, in front, eight small chairs and a table made for the children

♛ The Durbar Room *right* dates from 1890. It is designed in Indian style to commemorate the Queen's possessions in India

♔ In the Horn Room *above* nearly all the furniture is made of the antlers of deer – even the table-tops are inlaid with sections of horn. The pictures show the Queen's animals

♔ The Queen's Sitting Room *below* is decorated just as it was in Victoria's day, and is typical of English furnishing of the period. The twin writing tables were both used by Prince Albert

♛ The Queen's Bedroom has a canopied bed and a chintz sofa. Eight small busts of her children line the mantelpiece

♛ The Grand Staircase, leading to the Private Apartments, was decorated with paintings and marble statuary in the monumental style that was the current fashion

♛ After his death, the Prince's Writing Room *left* was kept exactly as it was in his lifetime. Many of the things he used are precisely where he left them. These include his umbrella and walking sticks, his dispatch box and writing materials – the whole room reflects his personal taste. The pictures, too, were chosen by the Prince himself

⚜ The Drawing Room *left*, overlooking the East Terrace, is decorated in blue, white and gold. Around the room are life-sized statues of the royal children. The grand piano and wall cabinets are of tulip wood, inlaid with plaques of Wedgwood jasper ware. The marble fireplace with its French clock is flanked by five-foot tall vases in gold and glass

⚜ In the Prince's Bathroom *right* are pictures painted by Prince Albert and some early photographs of the dramatic tableaux acted by the royal children

English Heritage

English Heritage

⚜ The Billiard Room *above* provided a retreat for the gentlemen of the household, and was out of sight of the adjacent Drawing Room. The elaborate painted decoration on the billiard table was designed by Prince Albert

⚜ Queen Victoria loved the gardens at Osborne. The photograph *left* was taken in May 1887. The Queen is shown taking tea with her guests in the shade of a vast canopy and attended by her devoted Indian servants

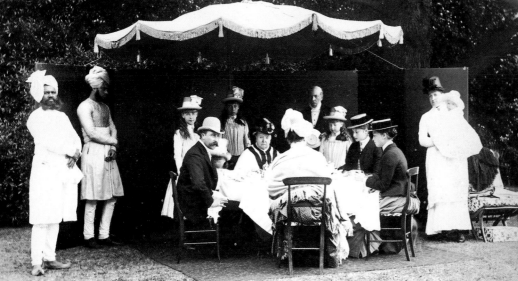

By gracious permission of HM the Queen

MY BELOVED ALBERT

THE GREAT EXHIBITION OF 1851 MARKED THE DAWNING OF A NEW AGE. BUT ALBERT'S PREMATURE DEATH WAS TO LEAVE VICTORIA A WIDOW AT 42

JUST OVER TEN YEARS AFTER VICTORIA AND Albert were married, London saw Albert's most public triumph – the Great Exhibition of 1851. Albert had never won general popularity, and Victoria believed that this brainchild of his would prove to the nation – and the world – Albert's exalted worth.

The opening day was 1 May 1851. Victoria wrote: 'this day is one of the greatest and most glorious days of our lives, with which, to my pride and joy, the name of my dearly beloved Albert is forever associated'.

It was Victoria who opened the world's first international exhibition – in the newly built Crystal Palace in Hyde Park.

Victoria described the scene vividly in her journal: 'The park presented a wonderful

A CROWNING ACHIEVEMENT

The Great Exhibition of 1851 was Albert's crowning achievement. The project was envisaged as a monument to peace, progress, prosperity and the unity of mankind, containing exhibits of the very best in the arts, sciences and industry from all over the world. All this was housed under one giant roof – a magnificent glass building spanning a total area of 18 acres, designed by the architect Joseph Paxton and built especially for the occasion. 'Its immense size,' wrote one observer, 'gives one a feeling of hopeless bewilderment.' One particular problem encountered by the designers of the exhibition was the preservation of the old elm trees on the envisaged site, Hyde Park. Paxton was able to overcome the problem by designing a vaulted rather than a flat roof, in which the trees could be centrally contained.

During the six months of the Exhibition's existence, over six million visitors came to study the exhibits. They included working class and poor people, who took advantage of the fact that two days a week the entrance fee was reduced, at Albert's suggestion, from two guineas to a shilling

Museum of London

spectacle, crowds streaming through it. The day was bright and all bustle and excitement. Vicky and Bertie were in our carriage. Vicky was dressed in lace over white satin with a small wreath of pink wild roses in her hair and looked very nice. Bertie was in full Highland dress. The Green Park and Hyde Park were one mass of densely crowded human beings in the highest good humour and most enthusiastic. The glimpse through the iron gates of the Transept, the moving palms and flowers, the myriads of people filling the galleries and seats around, together with the flourish of trumpets as we entered the building, gave a sensation I shall never forget, and I felt much moved.'

Albert's achievements

From the start Albert had been the guiding force, if not the instigator, of this ambitious project. The great hall was specially built for the occasion, and filled with exhibits of the best of the inventions and products of many countries. Despite alarms and grumbles, it was to be thrown open to the public. Throughout the two years of preparation for the event, he had been disappointed but unsurprised to encounter opposition from everyone, it seemed, but those involved in mounting the exhibition. No public money was granted for the financing of the project, and Albert had to raise the necessary capital from private investors. Experts and eminent people, who should have known better, prophesied complete disaster in the wake of the exhibition.

Albert wrote wryly of just some of the things that had been said: 'Mathematicians have calculated that the Crystal Palace will blow down in the first strong gale; Engineers that the galleries would crash in and destroy the visitors; Political Economists have prophesied a scarcity of food in London owing to the vast concourse of people; Doctors that owing to so many races coming into contact with each other, the Black Death of the Middle Ages would make its appearance as it did after the Crusades; Moralists that England would be affected by all the scourges of the civilised and uncivilised world; Theologians that this second Tower of Babel would draw upon it the vengeance of an offended God.'

The project was, nevertheless, a resounding success – achieving more than Victoria and

☒ *Many articles, such as the fan and medal above, were produced to commemorate the Great Exhibition. The medal shown at the top was made in the Machinery Courts of the Exhibition itself – an area of particular fascination for Queen Victoria*

Fotomas Index

Fotomas Index

LIFE AT BALMORAL

Balmoral House – a small residence near Braemar, Aberdeenshire – was to be Victoria and Albert's favourite summer retreat for many years. Here, the royal couple could relax completely, with only their children and two gillies for company. Glorious days were spent sketching, walking in the countryside, hunting, and visiting the local cottagers

Most exciting of all were the group expeditions with friends, traversing mountains and rivers, that would often last for several days at a time. To Victoria, Balmoral House and its surroundings was perfection itself. In her journal she was to write, 'Every year my heart becomes more fixed in this dear paradise'

National Army Museum

Albert even dreamed. At the close of the Exhibition, on 15 October (the twelfth anniversary of Victoria and Albert's engagement) over £180,000 profit remained – a huge fortune in those days, almost twice the sum that had been expected.

With this money, Albert was able to realize a more long-lasting dream: to develop a group of educational institutions that would benefit from the capital after his lifetime. Albert arranged for a large tract of land in Kensington Gore near the exhibition to be bought. Over the years, this site saw the erection of a number of memorials to the Prince: the Natural History Museum, the Science Museum, the Victoria and Albert Museum, the Royal Colleges of Art and Music and the Imperial College.

To Victoria, above all, the Great Exhibition had been of prime importance – not because of its commercial success but because of the personal glory it bestowed on her beloved husband. She later recalled its opening with pride: 'It was the *happiest, proudest* day in my life, and I can think of nothing else. Albert's dearest name is immortalized with this *great* conception, *his* own, and my *own* dear country *showed* she was worthy of it.'

A Highland retreat

Meanwhile, Victoria and Albert continued to value their escapist life at Balmoral. In 1852, after four years of renting Balmoral House close to the River Dee in the Highlands, Albert decided that it was time to buy the place they had fallen in love with. The old building needed substantial work, and Albert had it rebuilt to his own specifications.

The décor was a joint effort by Victoria and Albert, and somewhat startling. Every room was festooned with Victoria's own tartan: curtains, tartan chair-covers, tartan rugs – and even tartan lino on the floor. Stags' antlers were hung on many of the walls, and the lamps were bronze figurines of kilted Highlanders.

Victoria came to enjoy the visits she paid to the locals in the Highlands more and more. She was impressed and amused by how they treated her – with very little ceremony. Once, Victoria took her knitting with her to a cottage, where she was to pass some time with an old peasant woman. Suddenly, the old lady picked up the Queen's work, inspected it, and passed it back, saying dourly that she pitied the 'gude mon' if he had 'no better stockings than that'.

It was experiences like this that prompted Victoria and Albert to take trips through the Highlands incognito with a couple of friends and two servants. Victoria loved the subterfuge, especially when one of the servants nearly gave the game away by calling her 'Your Majesty' and Albert 'Your Royal Highness' – 'which set us off laughing, but no one observed it'. She was less amused, though, when they turned up at an inn to find there was hardly anything to eat. 'There was only tea, and two miserable starved Highland chickens without any potatoes! No pudding, and no fun.'

The Crimean War

In February 1854, Britain and France declared war on Russia, following the latter's invasion of Turkey, and the Crimean War had begun. Two years of fighting were to follow, and the Queen was unstinting in her praise of her 'dear soldiers'. These years also saw an improvement in the previously strained relations between England and France. In April 1855, Emperor Napoleon III and his wife Eugénie came to London, where they received a truly magnificent welcome. The visit was seen as a huge diplomatic success and in August 1855 there was a return visit by the English royal family to Paris – the first visit of an English sovereign for over 400 years.

During the war years, apart from her distress as monarch, Victoria suffered a private anguish when she heard that rumours were circulating about Albert. It was said that he was a Russian spy, and that he had been locked in the Tower of London. Crowds turned up outside the Tower and craned to catch a glimpse of the traitor. The Queen wrote bitterly: 'In attacking the Prince, who is one and the same with the Queen herself, the throne is assailed.'

But ironically it was the Crimean War that established Albert's reputation as a diplomat and gained him the respect of the British government. He advised on the reorganization of the army and the planning of campaigns – and his advice was respected and followed. Lord Palmerston spoke for many when he said, 'The Prince is a far greater and more extraordinary man than the Emperor.'

From this time on, the Prince's workload

Queen Victoria greatly admired the bravery of her soldiers at the Crimea, and met many of the wounded. It was in acknowledgement of their heroism that she was to institute the Victoria Cross medal in 1856 – to this day awarded for outstanding valour in the face of the enemy. Below Medals to commemorate the Franco-British alliance during the war

'My heart beats for them as for my nearest and dearest'

QUEEN VICTORIA, ON THE CRIMEAN SOLDIERS

increased. He could come out from behind the shadow of his wife and be respected for himself. He was constantly at meetings, attending councils of war, writing hundreds of memoranda, or going over state papers together with Victoria. Albert was always busy – it became normal for him to feel worn out, but this was what he had been educated for – one of the main reasons he married Victoria – and his sense of duty only caused him to work harder. Victoria often worried about the effect the work was having on him, saying that she 'was always so vexed and nervous if I had any foolish draft or despatch to show him as I knew it would distress and irritate him and affect his poor dear stomach'.

Albert's concerns were not just political. He was involved in overseeing the building of model houses for workmen, reorganizing the syllabus at Cambridge to include the humanities and science as well as Latin and Greek, and devising efficient sewerage systems and cleaning up the River Thames. He also designed a revolutionary sliding mirror for a drawing room at Osborne and a new milling machine for use on the royal farms.

Prince Consort

On 25 June 1857, Victoria was at last able to give her husband the title of Prince Consort of the United Kingdom of Great Britain and Ireland. 'Now I have a legal status in the English hierarchy,' Albert wrote, with some humour, to his stepmother. More important, as far as Victoria was concerned, it now meant that when they travelled abroad, Albert was accorded his rightful precedence, rather than having to take his place below minor royalty. To Victoria, there was no more important person in the world than her husband.

For as the years passed, Victoria's love and respect for Albert only deepened. There was never disillusionment, only fresh wonder at his goodness, beauty and talents. As Greville noted, 'Her devotion and submission know no bounds.'

Victoria hated to be away from Albert even for a day, and she loved nothing more than spending time alone with him. Indeed, when her eldest daughter Vicky married Prince Frederick of Prussia in 1858, Victoria felt some relief, because as the Princess Royal had grown older she had spent more time with her parents, leaving them less time to themselves. 'I find no especial pleasure or compensation in the company of the elder children,' Victoria wrote to a friend.

Victoria most loved being with Albert at Osborne, the small estate on the Isle of Wight

which they had bought soon after their marriage, or at Balmoral. She found his beauty undiminished, even as he started to grow bald and accumulate weight on that previously perfect figure.

In the country, they were both called at seven o'clock. Albert rose immediately to work, going straight through to his desk, only pausing to put on his dressing-gown, and sometimes a wig to keep his head warm indoors in the winter. Albert felt the cold more than Victoria, and he would often insist on having a fire lit. Victoria would have disapproved if anyone else had asked. She was strict about fires, only liking them lit in deep winter – and then only

The art of photography was still in its infancy during the 1850s – pictures were often posed and exaggerated. In one of the first pictures ever taken of the Queen and the Prince, Albert proudly displayed his Order of the Garter and Victoria wore her favourite lace dress. Yet the effect of the royal couple holding hands across a pillar is curiously romantic

A GRAND ALLIANCE

When Victoria visited Paris with Albert on 18 August 1855, she was the first British monarch to do so since the infant Henry VI was crowned there in 1430. The crowds were ecstatic in their welcome, and the visit was seen as a symbol of the newly acclaimed alliance between Britain and France

beech-wood as she had 'the same rooted objection to coal as to gas'.

After working for a while, Albert would dress for breakfast. He liked wearing bright waistcoats – so much so, that Victoria's mother usually made sure she bought him one at Christmas. Underneath, Albert always wore the Order of the Garter. At breakfast, he would read *The Times*, marking passages for Victoria. The family knew better than to disturb him at this one quiet moment of the day.

During the day, when Albert was not deep in his work, they would sometimes take walks together as a family, Albert followed by a line of little ones in height order. Sometimes at the end of the day, Victoria and Albert would go fishing for trout together in a rowing boat until darkness fell.

In the evenings, there was a reversal in their habits; earlier in their marriage it was Victoria who had liked to sit up till all hours. Now, sometimes when 11 o'clock came round, Albert was still in his study, while the Queen was ready for bed. A number of times she felt compelled to say, 'Tell Lord Alfred to let the Prince know that it is 11 o'clock. Tell him the Prince should merely be told the hour. The Prince wishes to be told, I know. He does not see the clock.'

On 14 April 1857, Princess Beatrice, their last child – known as 'Baby' – was born. Her doctor had been worried about Victoria having another child, partly because she dreaded it so

♛ *Amateur theatricals and tableaux were a feature of life at Windsor. In the Tableau of the Seasons above Princess Alice can be seen as Spring left, Princess Victoria and Prince Arthur as Summer, Prince Alfred centre as Autumn, the Prince of Wales and Princess Louise as Winter, and Princess Helena standing as the Spirit of the Empress Helena. Victoria and Albert also delighted in dressing up. In the picture right they are shown hosting a 'Restoration Ball' wearing costumes of the times of Charles II*

much herself. She had said 'she felt sure if she had another child she would sink under it'. Now, he informed her that it would be wise if she had no more children. Victoria is said to have enquired with much emotion whether that meant she could have 'no more fun with Albert'. The love she felt for him was as passionate and romantic as ever.

February 1861 saw the twenty-first anniversary of the royal couple's wedding. Victoria wrote in her usual frank and artless way to Uncle Leopold, 'Very few can say with me that their husband at the end of 21 years is not only full of the friendship, kindness, and affection which a truly happy marriage brings with it, but the same tender love of the very first days of our marriage.' She was supremely happy.

DEATH OF THE CONSORT

By gracious permission of HM the Queen

👑 *When Princess Victoria married Prince Frederick of Prussia on 25 January 1858, Victoria and Albert, while rejoicing at their 'Vicky's' happiness, were clearly sorry to lose their eldest daughter. The Queen confessed to feeling great nervousness on the day of the wedding, and was trembling so much when this picture was taken before the ceremony that the photograph was blurred. Within a few months, Victoria was to admit feeling 'delight' that she and Albert could at last dine alone. Her delight was not to last long. Years of overwork had taken their toll on Albert's health, and in 1861 he finally succumbed to typhoid. The picture on the right – one of the last representations of him – shows the Prince, typically, working even during his sickness*

Early in 1861, the bleakest period of Victoria's life began. In March, her mother died. Over the years, Victoria had come to love her mother. She realized that their relationship had been poisoned by Conroy and Lehzen, and she bitterly regretted the harsh things she had thought and written about her in her diary. Her sorrow was almost mad in its intensity, compounded by the guilt she felt and the opportunities lost to make up to her mother for the past. 'I love to dwell on her … and not be roused out of my grief.' The impact of her mother's death caused what can now be seen to be a nervous breakdown. Albert was also affected by the Duchess's death, and it made him contemplate his own.

Bertie's indiscretions

Later that year, both Victoria and Albert were profoundly shocked to find that Bertie, the Prince of Wales, had had an affair with an actress at the army camp where he was stationed. Albert was shattered. He said that the incident 'has caused me the greatest pain I have yet felt in my life'. On 25 November he visited Bertie, who was now at Cambridge, and they went some way to patching up this agonizing rift. But a day or two before, Albert had caught a chill. He was already weakened by overwork, and appalled and depressed by what he saw as his failure with Bertie, and his son's moral bankruptcy. He was now suffering from gastric trouble and insomnia, and he soon became seriously ill.

The doctors diagnosed his illness as a 'feverish sort of influenza', and he took to his bed at Windsor. Although Victoria was deeply worried, she was not immediately frightened.

Albert had not been well for at least two years: his diary had carried meticulous references to his state of health. For years, he had been what would now be termed a workaholic, although he would only have seen it as doing his duty. As soon as he had partially recovered from any illness, he would be up and working again — never giving his system time to recuperate thoroughly. There was no doubt that his health was damaged by overwork.

Typically, when he was feeling slightly better, Albert had work brought to him. On 1 December, Albert amended a memorandum that the Foreign Office had proposed sending to the American Government following an incident at

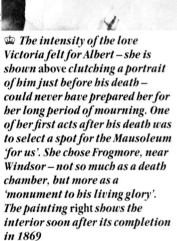

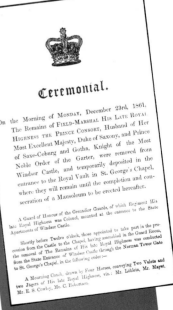

The Mansell Collection

♛ *The intensity of the love Victoria felt for Albert – she is shown* above *clutching a portrait of him just before his death – could never have prepared her for her long period of mourning. One of her first acts after his death was to select a spot for the Mausoleum 'for us'. She chose Frogmore, near Windsor – not so much as a death chamber, but more as a 'monument to his living glory'. The painting* right *shows the interior soon after its completion in 1869*

sea. He softened the tone to such an extent that he probably single-handedly averted a war with America. It was his last service to the country that during his life never fully appreciated him. He was dreadfully weak – 'I could hardly hold my pen', he said.

Before long, it became clear that his illness was very serious. It was soon realized that he had typhoid. It is ironic that he had worked to improve drainage yet it was the bad drains at Windsor Castle, 'frequently so exceedingly offensive as to render many parts of the Castle almost uninhabitable' that almost certainly had given him this dangerous, terminal illness.

By 7 December, Albert's mind was rambling, and his fever was dangerous.

The Queen called Princess Alice and Princess Helena to keep her company. On 13 December, Bertie arrived. Victoria had not wanted him there as she had become convinced that it was his debauchery that had caused Albert's fever.

It was years before Victoria could describe

the events of the next day. 'It was a bright morning, the sun just rising and shining brightly. The room had the sad look of night-watching, the candles burnt down to their sockets, the doctors looked anxious. I went in, and never can I forget how beautiful my darling looked lying there with his face lit up by the rising sun, his eyes unusually bright . . .'

The Prince's last breath

That evening, the family who were there gathered at Albert's bed. Victoria knelt at one side holding Albert's hand, facing Princess Alice. Princess Helena knelt with Bertie at the foot of the bed. 'Two or three long but perfectly gentle breaths were drawn, the hand clasping mine and . . . all, all, was over . . . I stood up, kissed his dear heavenly forehead and called out in a bitter and agonizing cry, "Oh! my dear Darling!"'

It was 10.50 on 14 December 1861. Albert had died, and Victoria embarked on her 40 years of mourning.

A MARRIAGE REMEMBERED

Part of the legacy of Victoria's love for Albert is an array of loving mementoes. Among them are the lockets and pictures they gave each other, together with their most valued possessions from childhood. They also include Victoria's own paintings and sketches which intimately chronicle her life before and after her beloved Albert's death

By gracious permission of HM the Queen

👑 Two of Victoria's sketches capture the lovers at the height of their romance. The self-portrait was drawn just before her 26th birthday and the watercolour of Albert was painted in 1845

Museum of London

♛ Victoria commissioned the lovely painting *above* from her favourite artist, Franz Xavier Winterhalter, as a surprise present for Albert's 24th birthday on 26 August 1843. Deliberately intimate and informal, a long tress of hair hangs across her bare shoulder. Albert was delighted with the picture which was placed in his Writing Room at Windsor. *Left*. 30 years later, at Balmoral, a flower-decked table was laden with gifts for the Queen on her 54th birthday. The picture of Albert still dominates 12 years after his death

♛ The gold locket *left* is said to have been given to John Brown by Queen Victoria. It holds portraits of Victoria and Albert, their initials and locks of hair. The memorial ring *right* was set with a portrait of the Prince. Victoria wore it until her death.

Museum of London

By gracious permission of HM the Queen

English Heritage

By gracious permission of HM the Queen

♛ The wooden dolls *far left* are from Victoria's famous collection, started when she was a young girl. With the help of her governess, Lehzen, she dressed 132 of them. The German musical box *bottom left* was a Christmas present from Prince Albert to his children.

The Queen was a talented artist as shown *above* by this family scene, painted at Osborne House in 1850. The self-portrait was sketched after her typhoid attack in 1835 and the child's portrait *left* is of her youngest daughter, Beatrice. *Top right* is a rare photograph of Queen Victoria, seen smiling faintly. With her is her favourite collie, Sharp.

The room in Windsor Castle *below right* is where Prince Albert died of typhoid on 14 December 1861. The room was left untouched until Victoria died

♛ *Albert was gone but not forgotten. His presence was everywhere right and Victoria looked to him in death as she had in life – with adoration. Memorials commemorating his wide range of interests dotted the British landscape, from rural Balmoral below right to fashionable Kensington*

LASTING MEMORIAL

LIFE WITHOUT ALBERT SEEMED UNBEARABLE, AND FOR A WHILE VICTORIA'S MOURNING TOOK ON AN ALMOST SPIRITUAL INTENSITY. BUT TIME EASED THE PAIN, AND TOWARDS THE END OF HER REIGN, THE EMPIRE SALUTED A BELOVED QUEEN AT HER DIAMOND JUBILEE

VICTORIA WAS, LITERALLY, STUNNED BY Albert's death. She thought she was losing her mind, and perhaps hoped that if she could not, she would die immediately herself.

Every morning, 'Baby' Princess Beatrice was brought to her bedroom to greet her when she was woken, so that she would have the comforting presence of a bright four-year-old. But she was completely frozen in her grief.

After Albert's death, everyone at the court had to wear full mourning for a year; the servants continued to wear black crêpe mourning bands on their arms for another eight years. The ladies-in-waiting wore mourning till 1864, after which they were allowed a restricted range of dresses in grey, violet or white. The chief lady-in-waiting, however, was told that she had to continue to wear mourning as long as the Queen did. But there never came a moment when Victoria could say that mourning was over; she wore her black widow's clothes till the end of her life.

Perpetual bereavement

For 40 years, at the Queen's command, hot water and fresh clothes were laid out in Albert's room every evening; in the morning his chamberpot was taken away and scrubbed with the rest. In every way, except his physical presence, Albert remained vividly alive for Victoria. Indeed, before she signed a document of State, she would look up at a bust of Albert and ask him if he approved.

In March 1863, her son and heir, Bertie, married Princess Alexandra of Denmark. Victoria adored 'Alix' and felt Bertie was lucky to have her. But although it was well over a year since Albert's death, she was still engulfed by her grief and found it impossible to enjoy the day. 'At one moment, when I first heard the flourish of trumpets, which brought back to my mind my whole life of 20 years at his dear side, safe, proud, secure, and happy, I felt as if I should faint. Only by a violent effort could I succeed in mastering my emotion.'

At first, the whole nation felt nothing but sympathy for the Queen who had lost her much-loved husband so young. But as the years passed, and she showed no sign of wanting to lift herself from her grief, the country's patience began to run out. She shunned public duties and showed herself in public as little as possible. People grumbled among themselves and newspapers openly criticized her bizarre seclusion.

Lasting comfort

Malicious rumours even circulated about her relationship with one of her Scottish servants, the gillie John Brown, who had been a favourite with Victoria and Albert. Soon after Albert's death, he was asked to bring her favourite pony to the Queen, in the hope that she would leave her rooms for some exercise.

John Brown soon became invaluable to her. He had the rough, frank Highland manners that she admired and, unlike other servants, he was not ambitious. Apart from his passion for whisky, which would occasionally send him about his duties reeling drunk, he was devoted to the Queen, and she knew she could trust him totally. He could speak frankly to Victoria, and, sometimes, was able to persuade her to do things when everyone else had failed – which hardly endeared him to his colleagues. In fact, he was almost universally detested. Lord Ponsonby, her private secretary, while not liking

Ghenar Freres/By gracious permission of HM the Queen

♛ *Victoria grieved with a passion that reached monumental extremes. Notepaper and handkerchiefs acquired extra-thick black borders, and mourning was the only attire she would allow to be worn at court. The widow's weeds she took to were never forsaken for the rest of her life*

☙ *Victoria always needed the support of a strong man. After Albert's death, she looked increasingly to the ministrations of John Brown, her Scottish servant top. His brusque intimacy was resented by Court and family alike but Victoria felt utterly protected and comfortable with him. Once, when sensing her weariness at a welcoming ceremony at Coburg, when the drumming proved too loud, Brown ended the ceremony peremptorily with a 'Nix boom boom' to the officer. Disraeli, Victoria's favourite Prime Minister above, was just the opposite. Oozing urbane charm, he flattered her out of her melancholy and gave her confidence as monarch – not least, when he presented her with the Crown of India. She, in turn, created him Lord Beaconsfield*

Brown personally, admitted that he was 'a most excellent servant' to Victoria, and so put up with him. As she herself said, he was 'groom, footman, page and maid' to her. The papers sneered, saying that they were secretly married and openly called Victoria 'Mrs John Brown'.

But Victoria refused to worry about what other people thought. She desperately needed people on whom she could lean. In 1867, on the anniversary of her succession, Victoria wrote in her journal, 'I have been 30 years in harness and therefore ought to know what should be – but I am *terribly shy* and nervous and *always was so*.'

Then at the end of 1871, close to the tenth anniversary of Albert's death, Bertie, too, went down with typhoid fever. For a while, he was dangerously ill.

Victoria's new cause for worry and grief heralded a turn-around in her popularity. 'The feeling shown by the whole nation is quite marvellous and most touching and striking, showing how truly loyal the people really are.'

Her other 'favourite'

Following Bertie's slow recovery, something else happened that set the seal on Victoria's new-won popularity. On leap-day in 1872, a young man tried to shoot her while she was out in her carriage. John Brown noticed him and wrestled him to the ground before he was able to fire. During her reign, she suffered five other attempts on her life but this one – so soon after she had nearly lost her heir – brought her subjects closer to her and they started to value their Queen – in spite of her many foibles.

Her ministers and her household soon came to adapt themselves to her idiosyncrasies. Disraeli, who became her favourite Prime Minister in a relationship that was almost romantic, said, 'Everyone likes flattery; when you come to royalty, you should lay it on with a trowel.' But he never underestimated the Queen of whom he was really fond. Victoria wrote that he was 'full of poetry, romance and chivalry. When he knelt down to kiss my hand

which he took in both his – he said, "In loving loyalty and faith".' Disraeli had discovered the secret: he treated Victoria like a woman, as well as a Queen.

But the Liberal Prime Minister, Gladstone, was never to have the same success. His intense dedication unnerved her and his foreign policies positively repelled her, so that when, in 1880, he was to succeed Disraeli, she tried her best – almost unconstitutionally – to obstruct his appointment.

The pall of gloom

Her difficult behaviour spread. Where she had previously revelled in other people's romances, now that Albert was dead she disapproved of any of her household getting married. Dr James Reid, who became Resident Physician in 1881, annoyed her by announcing his engagement to one of her Maids-of-Honour, the Honourable Susan Baring. Eventually, she forgave him because he amused her by promising 'never to do it again'.

In 1876, to her great pride, Victoria became Empress of India. She loved all things Indian, and later surrounded herself with Indian servants. She also learnt Hindustani so that she could speak to them and, as she said to her Governor-General, Lord Canning, there should be 'no hatred of brown skin'.

Social life at Balmoral, which had once been interspersed with entertainment and fun, now became something to be dreaded. As Victoria preferred to be surrounded by people she knew, those in attendance started to grow old, and some of them were severely deaf – which meant that small-talk was desultory or non-existent. Invitations to dinners at Balmoral were accepted with gloom. They were 'appallingly dull' and the 'most depressing functions' Ponsonby had ever known.

After dinner, the ladies would usually sit quietly playing patience while the Queen sat silently sipping coffee from a cup whose saucer was held by an Indian servant.

Very occasionally, the Queen was in a jolly mood and 'seemed prepared for prattle'. Her most adoring grandson, who was to become Kaiser Wilhelm II of Germany, told of the time Victoria was having a conversation with an admiral about a ship. Tiring of the topic, the Queen changed the subject and asked after the admiral's sister. He was rather deaf and misheard the question, and continued on the same tack as before. 'Well, Ma'am,' he said, 'I'm going to have her turned over and take a good look at her bottom and have it well scraped.'

'The effect of this answer was stupendous', the Kaiser wrote. 'My grandmother put down